CONTENTS

Hoax Horse Rap

Hey, everybody,
don't snooze and snore.
I'm gonna tell the story
of the Trojan War.

Tony Mitton

MIGHTY GREEK MYTH RAPS

Illustrated by Martin Chatterton

 ORCHARD BOOKS

To Mary, Michael, Joe and the dog Parsnip
T.M.

ORCHARD BOOKS
96 Leonard Street, London, EC2A 4XD
Orchard Books Australia
Unit 31/56 O'Riordan Street, Alexandria, Sydney, NSW 2015
First published in Great Britain in 2001
First paperback edition 2002
Text © Tony Mitton 2001
Illustrations © Martin Chatterton 2001
The rights of Tony Mitton to be identified as the author
and Martin Chatterton as the illustrator of this work
have been asserted by them in accordance with the
Copyright, Designs and Patents Act, 1988.
A CIP catalogue record for this book is available
from the British Library.
ISBN 1 84121 809 X (hardback)
ISBN 1 84121 811 1 (paperback)
1 3 5 7 9 10 8 6 4 2 (hardback)
1 3 5 7 9 10 8 6 4 2 (paperback)
Printed in Great Britain

It started when Helen,
a young Greek queen
(the greatest beauty
that ever was seen)
got pulled by Paris,
Prince of Troy.
Her husband, Menelaus,
cried,

He launched his
fighting ships - *ahoy!*
Then he sailed with his army
off to Troy.

The walls of Troy
were tall and stout,
and they kept those Greek guys
firmly out.
But the Trojans often
slipped outside
to fight on the plain
with puffed-up pride.

TROY

Queen Helen was there,
high up in a tower,
watching the fighting
hour by hour.

They fought for days,
they fought for weeks,
with bows and arrows,
howls and shrieks.
They fought for months,
they fought for years,
with spears and shields,
shouts and jeers.

But neither Greeks
nor Trojans won,
and nobody
was having fun.

So smart Odysseus,
feeling bored,
put down his shield
and sheathed his sword.

This clever Greek
was sharp and shrewd,
a very cool
and cunning dude.
He cried, "Eureka!
Yes, of course!
We'll build a great big
wooden horse."

His mates thought he'd
gone off his trolley.
But later on,
they murmured, "Golly!
That's a really
clever plan.
How'd you think
of that one, man?"

They fetched their tools
and planks of wood...

...and made a horse
as best they could.

But not a horse
you'd try to ride -
a horse for hiding
men inside!

The Greeks picked out
their bravest force
who hid themselves
inside the horse.

This wooden horse
so fine and tall,
they left it near
the Trojan wall.

The Trojans frowned.
"What can this mean?
Is this some kind
of war machine?
But look down there.
Now ain't that hip?
Those grotty Greeks
are boarding ship!"

13

They watched the Greek ships
sail away.
Then suddenly they cheered,
"Hooray!
Those greasy geeks
have had enough.
They've found us Trojans
far too tough.

The horse must be
some kind of sign
to say, 'OK, guys,
we resign.'
Or maybe it's
some sort of present,
a Greek attempt
at being pleasant.

Anyway,
the Greeks have gone.
So, come on, Troy,
let's party on!"

So, glad the war
was done at last,
the Trojans dropped
their weapons fast.

The Trojans felt
so big and brave
they had a mega
midnight rave.

17

And then they stumbled
off to bed,
and mumbled, "Man!
I'm almost dead…"

And they were right,
for, as they slept,
those sneaky Greek guys
quietly crept.
They left the horse,
unlocked Troy's gate
and settled down -
not long to wait.

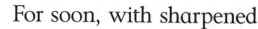

For soon, with sharpened
spear tips,
the Greeks returned
with all their ships.
Sailing off
had been a trick.
They'd sailed back
by night, real quick.

They tiptoed straight up
from the shore,
and gave their sleeping
foes what for.

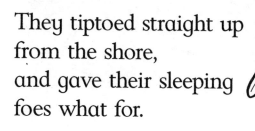

They chased them shrieking
from the town,
then burned the whole
caboodle down.
Till Troy, that city,
once so proud,
was ashes in
a smoking cloud.

And Menelaus
got back his queen.

"I told you not
to talk to strangers.
Didn't I say
it's full of dangers?
I hope, from now,
that you'll behave.
But - *whoop!* - we won!
Let's hold a rave!"

Round Eye Rap

After his trick
with the wooden horse
Odysseus' ship
got blown off course.

He was trying to sail
to Greece from Troy,
but he wasn't getting
too much joy.
And when, at last,
the wind dropped away,
they'd come to an isle
with a quiet bay.

They were out of food.
They needed more.
So Odysseus said,
"We'll go ashore.
But I'm not the kind
of guy who begs,
so we'll trade some wine.
Let's take two kegs.

We'll swap the wine
for meat and bread,
and then we'll sail
for home, well fed."

High on the cliffs,
yes, way up there,
were caves, and it looked
like folk lived there.
So they visited one
and waited to see
who the owner might
turn out to be.

25

Well, quite soon, in
came a flock of sheep,
and it made the sailors'
brave hearts leap!
'Cos every sheep
was the size of a cow.
Odysseus murmured,

The shepherd did
come in at last.

And - *phew!* - that guy
was quite a size.
But just get this -
instead of eyes
set neatly in
the normal place,
he had just one eye
on his face!

And it was big
as a wagon wheel.
The sight of that
could make you squeal!

But Odysseus didn't
hesitate.
He called out, "Hey there!
Greetings, mate!
We've brought two kegs
of wine with us
to trade for food.
OK? No fuss?"

28

The shepherd gave
a nasty sneer,
and growled, "We don't
do trading here.
Us guys are Cyclops.
What we do
is feed on wimps
like *you* and *you!*"

He snatched two men
with sudden speed,
then gobbled them
with monstrous greed.
They had no time
to shriek or shout.
And then he spat
their armour out.

Odysseus thought,
I need a plan,
before he eats
another man.

"Good sir," he said,
"Our wine will waste.
So wash your meal down.
Try a taste.
My name is No One.
Be my guest.
Crack open a keg
of Trojan Best."

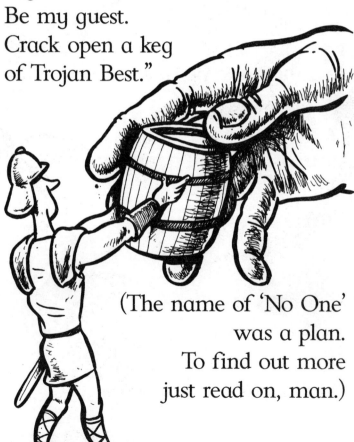

(The name of 'No One'
was a plan.
To find out more
just read on, man.)

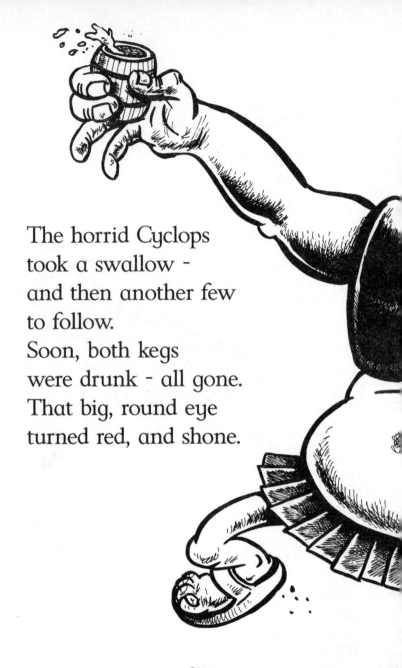

The horrid Cyclops
took a swallow -
and then another few
to follow.
Soon, both kegs
were drunk - all gone.
That big, round eye
turned red, and shone.

"Thank you, No One," droned the beast. "But now I'm dozy with that feast.

I'll settle down and take a sleep. You lot can stay here with my sheep. I'll trap you with my cavern door. Then, when I wake, I'll eat some more."

33

The door was huge -
a solid boulder.
The Cyclops shut it
with one shoulder.
Odysseus gave
a quiet groan.

We'll never move
that massive stone.

So, while the Cyclops
snored and shook,
Odysseus took
the shepherd's crook,
and sharpened it
into a spear
until it seemed
a thing to fear.

He fired the point
to make it hot,
to make it burn
and singe a lot.

Then twelve strong men
all held it high
and drove it through
the Cyclops' eye.

The monster gave
a massive roar
and knocked the men
upon the floor.
And then he made
a howling sound.
The monster's mates
came rushing round.

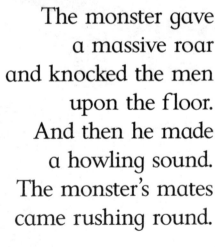

"He's had a dream,"
his mates all said.
"Or else he's gone
clean off his head.
If no one's hurt you,
what's the fuss?
Next time, please,
don't bother us."

His mates all stumbled
back to bed.
"Whoopee! It worked!"
Odysseus said.

38

The Cyclops gave
an angry sigh
and sat to nurse
his aching eye.

39

When morning came,
it wasn't long
before the sheep
felt something wrong.

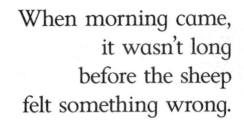

They filled the cave
with baa and bleat
as if to say,
"We need to eat.
We want some lovely,
juicy grass.
Please open up
and let us pass."

The Cyclops growled,
"My eye's gone dead,
but sheep like you
must still be fed.
These men may think
I cannot see.
But they won't make
a fool of me.

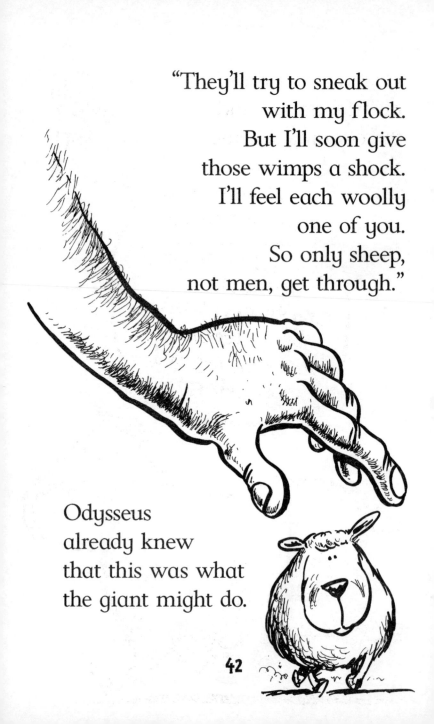

"They'll try to sneak out
with my flock.
But I'll soon give
those wimps a shock.
I'll feel each woolly
one of you.
So only sheep,
not men, get through."

Odysseus
already knew
that this was what
the giant might do.

42

He'd whispered to
his frightened band
the cunning scheme
that he had planned.

The sheep are big.
So you can hide
beneath their bellies,
and so ride
to safety, hidden
by a fleece.
And that way find,
I hope, release.

The Cyclops stroked
each fleecy pet
upon its back,
so failed to get
the men, that did
as they'd been bidden,
and that way stayed
entirely hidden.

When all of them
were out the cave,
Odysseus whispered,
"Phew! Close shave!
We'll drive some sheep
down to the bay,
then launch our ship
and get away."

No sailor needed
telling twice.
That island wasn't
very nice.

45

They drove aboard
a sheep or two -
enough to make
a mutton stew.

And then Odysseus
hissed, "Get going!"
For it was time
for nifty rowing.

46

Well, there you have
two tales that show
the world of Greece
so long ago.
But look, we're here,
beside the sea.
So come and take
a dip with me!

RAP RHYMES
by Tony Mitton
Illustrated by Martin Chatterton

Collect all the books in this award-winning series!

❏ 1 Royal Raps	ISBN 1 86039 366 7	£3.99
❏ 2 Big Bad Raps	ISBN 1 86039 365 9	£3.99
❏ 3 Fangtastic Raps	ISBN 1 86039 881 2	£3.99
❏ 4 Monster Raps	ISBN 1 86039 882 0	£3.99
❏ 5 Scary Raps	ISBN 1 84121 153 2	£3.99
❏ 6 Robin Hood Raps	ISBN 1 84121 157 5	£3.99

Look out for these Greek Myth Raps!

❏ 1 Mega Greek Myth Raps	ISBN 1 84121 803 0	£3.99
❏ 2 Groovy Greek Hero Raps	ISBN 1 84121 799 9	£3.99
❏ 3 Mighty Greek Myth Raps	ISBN 1 84121 811 1	£3.99
❏ 4 Great Greek Myth Raps	ISBN 1 84121 807 3	£3.99

Rap Rhymes are available from all good bookshops,
or can be ordered direct from the publisher:
Orchard Books, PO BOX 29, Douglas IM99 1BQ
Credit card orders please telephone 01624 836000 or fax 01624 837033
or e-mail: bookshop@enterprise.net for details.

To order please quote title, author and ISBN
and your full name and address.
Cheques and postal orders should be made payable to 'Bookpost plc'.
Postage and packing is FREE within the UK
(overseas customers should add £1.00 per book).

Prices and availability are subject to change.